Duck Hunting for Kids

A Comprehensive Guide to Make It a Fun Activity for the Young Hunters

Duck Hunting for Kids

2

© Copyright 2018

All rights reserved.

The content contained within this book may not be reproduced, duplicated or transmitted without direct written permission from the author or the publisher.

Under no circumstances will any blame or legal responsibility be held against the publisher, or author, for any damages, reparation, or monetary loss due to the information contained within this book. Either directly or indirectly.

Legal Notice:

This book is copyright protected. This book is only for personal use. You cannot amend, distribute, sell, use, quote or paraphrase any part, or the content within this book, without the consent of the author or publisher.

Duck Hunting for Kids

Disclaimer Notice:

Please note the information contained within this document is for educational and entertainment purposes only. All effort has been executed to present accurate, up to date, and reliable, complete information. No warranties of any kind are declared or implied. Readers acknowledge that the author is not engaging in the rendering of legal, financial, medical or professional advice. The content within this book has been derived from various sources. Please consult a licensed professional before attempting any techniques outlined in this book.

By reading this document, the reader agrees that under no circumstances is the author responsible for any losses, direct or indirect, which are incurred as a result of the use of information contained within this document, including, but not limited to, — errors, omissions, or inaccuracies.

Table Of Contents

Introduction 7
Chapter 1 – Why Duck Hunting is Fun 9
   Perfect bonding time: 11
      1. High Action Activity: 12
      2. Calling and Then Some More Calling: 12
      3. Cool Equipment: ....
      4. No Hassle to Conceal the Scent: ....
      5. Learning the Importance of Planning While Setting Up the Decoys: ....

Chapter 2 – Equipment to Bring ....
      1. Clothes as Per the Weather: 17
      2. Your Gun(s) and Their Licenses: 17
      3. Carry a Compass and Maps: 18
      4. A Camping Tent: 19
      5. Permission of the Landowner: 19
      6. First Aid Kit: ....
      7. Phone Chargers/Cables: ....
      8. Flashlight: ....
      9. Insects Spray/ Mosquito Repellent: ....
      10. Food and Snacks: ....
      11. Hunting Kit: ....

Chapter 3 – Tips and Tricks ....
      1. Wait Until Your Kids Are Ready: ....
      2. It's All about Fun: ....
      3. Equip Them With An Age-Appropriate Gun:
      4. Be Patient: ....
      5. Check the Weather Forecast: 28
      6. Break The Norm – Hunt The Ducks During Summertime: 28

7. Learn About The Land: 29
8. Waterproof Everything: 30
9. Protect the Ears With Muffs: 30
10. Scouting for the Ducks: 31
11. Empower your kids with responsibility: 32
12. Let them jump and catch the ducks: 32

Chapter 4 - Safety Measures 34
1. Visit a Shooting Range Before The Duck Hunt: 34
2. Keeping the Weapon at a Safe Distance from the Face: 35
3. Wearing a Life Jacket: 36
4. Respect the Shooting Lanes: 36
5. Carry a Waterproof Fire-Starting Kit: 37
Have Your Boat and Machinery Serviced: 37
Using a Boat of an Appropriate Size: 38
6. Equip Your Boat With Survival Gear: 38
7. Treat Your Gun as if it's loaded: 39
8. Have Your Gun(S) Serviced: 39
9. Carry licenses for all the weapons: 40

Chapter 5 – Animal Conservation 41
1. Read The Rules Every Single Time: 41
2. Daily Bag Limit: 42
3. Possession Limit: 42
4. Shooting Season and Hunting Hours: 43
5. Permits and license requirements: 43

Glossary of Common Terms 45

Introduction

No matter what the age, outdoor activities are always fun, especially when they are done together as a family. In the most subtle ways, you create precious memories that linger on forever. Whether it's hiking or camping, hunting or fishing, playing golf or quietly sitting under the sky in a starry night, each activity has its own charm and unfolds multiple bonding chances when shared with your loved ones.

Speaking of outdoor activities, many people are fond of waterfowl hunting. They don't want to miss any chance to go out, trek the fields, layout the decoys and hunt the waterfowl. It is a timeless passion and a rewarding sport, where the hunt is treated as a trophy and brings in the feeling of triumph and glory.

Although this sport is now not as common as it had been in the past - owing to our busy digital lifestyle - thanks to those few hunting enthusiasts who have still kept this golden tradition alive. They still love to indulge in this activity and share it with their friends, family, and children, despite the odd hours which can sometimes turn into a very long day.

Many people wonder what makes the hunting so intoxicating when you can watch the wildlife programs from the comfort of your own home and purchase every kind of meat right from the market. To them, it may be a waste of time, but for a hunter, it's an obsession that he'd not give up for anything in the world.

This book is dedicated to all the waterfowl hunting lovers, particularly the duck hunters, who wish to pass on this valuable tradition to their children. It is a comprehensive guide as to what to expect when you bring children along with you, and how to make this journey a memorable one for them.

Chapter 1 – Why Duck Hunting is Fun

When it comes to field sports, each huntsman has a personal preference regarding the choice of the hunt. While some enjoy following a deer across the forest, others find pleasure in shooting birds. Not only this, each type of hunting is further categorized into the species that one would like to go after. For example, if we talk about waterfowl hunting, there is a choice between geese, swans, and ducks.

Although many people love waterfowl hunting in general, there is a specific group of hunters that love duck hunting only. It is one of those activities that are enjoyed by everyone, regardless of the age; hence, most hunters love to teach their skills to their children.

So, what makes duck hunting so appealing to everyone?

For starters, looking at the spectacular beauty of the sky right before the sunrise, smelling the fresh scent of air just before dawn, witnessing the wonders of nature with your naked eye, and sharing these peaceful moments with your loved ones are just a few of the many perks that are enjoyed by duck hunters.

Duck hunters feel, see, observe and smell the things that cannot be experienced otherwise. After all, nothing can beat the thrill of going out there in the wild to find the flocks of birds passing by, and the feel of adrenaline rushing through your veins, the glorious feeling when a duck responds to your call and the shiver it sends down your spine. Last but not least, hunters get to enjoy their day's effort around a bonfire with their loved ones.

However, the bounties of duck hunting don't end here. The duck hunters know the value of their passion and they are almost always quite enthusiastic about getting their kids ready to take on the hunting when the time comes. Here are the reasons why duck hunters love to share their favorite sport with their kids, and why it is one of the most pleasurable outdoor activities:

Perfect bonding time:

Kids love to indulge in a sport that allows them to be both wild and free, and duck hunting is certainly one of the excellent ways to get them started. Unlike the other types of field sports, duck hunting doesn't require them to stay quiet. You won't need to hush your kids every now and then. As a matter of fact, you can spend your time having meaningful conversations with them and invoke positivity in their being. You can chat about their interests and what they want to do with their lives. Ultimately, this will help you in developing a deep bond with a memory that will stay with them all through their lives.

1. High Action Activity:

Duck hunting is an exhilarating experience for youngsters. It's a high-action activity where they can run around the fields to spot where ducks are landing, lay out decoys, generate calls to attract them, and then hopefully end up catching a few ducks.

The entire activity is spellbinding and fun-filling, which is a perfect match to a child's curious and active nature.

2. Calling and Then Some More Calling:

Nothing works better to attract waterfowl than calling. Every hunter knows that; hence, manufacturers have created special instruments to produce the calling sounds. Some hunters still prefer to imitate the quacking sounds themselves, while others take the support of calling instruments.

For duck hunting, there are at least 7 different types of calls that are used to capture a flying flock's attention, and, guess what? Kids love to make the calling sounds. They find it exciting, and perhaps if your kid is not big enough to handle a gun, maybe you can make him a calling-in-charge officer on your next hunt.

3. Cool Equipment:

The action-packed instruments and machinery required for duck hunting itself are a huge attraction, even for grown-ups. Motorboats, spinners, calls, and the decoys; the toys collection for this sport is huge, and is interesting enough to captivate children. They would not only love to use the hunting equipment on their excursion, but they will like to help you in cleaning and putting them away after an exciting trip.

4. No Hassle to Conceal the Scent:

Duck hunters, unlike deer hunters, don't need to be cautious about revealing their scents to the target. This means that a lot of work is cut down that otherwise comes in the form of taking a bath with a scent-free soap or spraying all over with a scent concealer. Some forms of hunting even require the huntsmen to put away the hunting clothes in an air-tight concealer, so they don't shoo away a potential target.

Thankfully, duck hunting doesn't require you to go these extra miles; hence, it is something you can easily share with your kids without any undue effort.

5. Learning the Importance of Planning While Setting Up the Decoys:

As insignificant as it may sound, setting up the decoys and traps for duck hunting requires some serious thinking, which, as a result, helps the youngsters to learn about strategic planning.

Ducks prefer to stay together and fly in groups as they feel safe this way. An incoming flock naturally tries to position itself in the center of a crowd while landing on the ground. This calls for some extra planning while laying out your decoys.

Decoys are usually arranged in a V or a U shape, while carefully keeping a space in the center of the set-up for the landing of the incoming ducks. This practice helps kids realize the importance of planning and making efficient use of every available resource.

Chapter 2 – Equipment to Bring

With the excitement of an upcoming hunting excursion with the kids, it's entirely understandable if you forget a thing or two; however, this minor mistake may be enough to spoil your entire fun. For example, what will happen if you forget to take something apparently as insignificant as a mosquito repellent? Well, you'll definitely find it really hard to focus on the game while dealing with the mosquito bites and the resultant itching.

However, don't worry! This guide is here to assist!

We have compiled an exhaustive list of all the things that you need to pack for your duck hunting trip, keeping in mind that you'll be taking your kids along. So, keep this list handy the next time you plan your hunt trip and voila – you're good to go.

1. Clothes as Per the Weather:

Weather-appropriate attire is an absolute must for duck hunting trips. You'll end up losing your energy fighting the weather if you feel too hot or too cold.

Another important thing is to clad yourself in waterproof clothing. Your outerwear, including the jacket, trousers, socks, and boots, should be entirely made of a waterproof material. The same goes for the kids who are joining you for the trip. They'll never be able to enjoy their hunting adventure if they feel wet and miserable.

If you are planning your hunt during winter, which is mostly the case for duck hunters, make sure to dress up in enough layers to keep your body warm in bone-chilling weather.

2. Your Gun(s) and Their Licenses:

You are going for a duck hunting trip, so most

likely you'll remember to keep your gun with you. However, also make sure to carry your gun license along with you, as you will most likely need to show them at a checkpoint. The same goes for your kid's firearms.

Some territories also require hunters to carry a Migratory Bird Hunting Permit before they are allowed to hunt. Make sure to check the rules and regulations in the area where you intend to hunt, and arrange all the necessary passes beforehand.

3. Carry a Compass and Maps:

No matter how confident you are about the site where you intend your duck hunt, it's always a good practice to carry a compass and a map of the territory where you are hunting.

It will not only help you to avoid getting lost, which is definitely something you don't want to happen while the kids are accompanying you, but it will also help you find nearby interesting spots that you can show to your children.

4. A Camping Tent:

It could be a simple hunting camp or an RV, but make sure that you take your temporary resting place along with you to make a home away from home. Even if you plan duck hunting during the day hours, you'll need a resting place to catch your breath and regain your energy.

Kids, especially, get tired easily, and a camp will help you avoid a big tantrum that could result if they get over-tired.

5. Permission of the Landowner:

If you are planning your duck hunting trip on private land, make sure to acquire the landowner's permission days ahead of time. You will most likely need to show the permission letter at the entry point to get access.

6. First Aid Kit:

It's a known fact that you cannot avoid cuts while you're on an outdoor adventure. However, hunters are more prone to getting hurt than any other outdoor sport, so it's very important to carry your first aid kit, particularly if you have kids as your companions.

Blood clutters, antiseptic, cotton roll and bandages are a few must-haves in your first aid box. Also, pack Tylenol or any other painkiller for immediate pain relief in case of an emergency.

Last, but not least, your first aid kit should contain any prescribed medicines for you and your hunting partners while you are going away from your home.

7. Phone Chargers/Cables:

You must be prepared to deal with any kind of emergency when taking your kids to a blood sports trip. You will ultimately require your cell phone in case of any mishap.

Make sure that your phone is fully charged before you leave home. Pack the charging cables in case your battery runs out during the trip. You can then always charge your phone via your car's battery.

8. Flashlight:

Good time flies by, and the same goes for hunting. It is really easy to lose track of the hours while you are out on duck hunting.

Always carry a flashlight and keep it in your carry bag so you don't run out of light if the sun sets in. Your emergency light will also come in handy if your hunting takes you deep in the woods.

If you are planning your trip for more than a day, pack extra batteries in your luggage to keep your flashlight working.

9. Insects Spray/ Mosquito Repellent:

A bug bite can cause a major discomfort. Moreover, having mosquitoes or insects buzzing around you while you are hunting is a huge turn-off.

To avoid this unpleasant situation and to fully focus on the game in hand, always carry an effective bug spray or mosquito repellent along with you. You can also keep bug bite medicine in your first aid kit for extra cover.

10. Food and Snacks:

Yes, you are going on a hunting trip, and you'll most likely be able to hunt something that you'd love to cook and eat.

However, you still need some snacks and hunt-friendly food to avoid hunger pangs while you are out at work.

Not only this, but your kids will also need to stay well fed to stay happy and focused. Make sure to pack their favorite snacks, and DON'T FORGET THE WATER!

11.Hunting Ki t:

Preferably a waterproof bag, your hunting kit will include duck calls, decoys, a waterproof fire-starting kit, flashlight, and water bottle.

You'll be carrying this hunting bag on the field away from your camp so take some time to plan its contents. Try keeping anything and everything that you think you'll need in the hunting area. You'll certainly dislike the idea of running back and forth between the camp and the hunting site for minor things.

Chapter 3 – Tips and Tricks

Duck hunting is a fascinating outdoor activity to involve your children in. It has everything to keep them on their toes (in a good way) – thrill, action, imitation of sounds, fun and a great result towards the end.

To add more excitement to your upcoming hunting trip and to reduce any hassle, here is a list of some recommended tips and tricks, as conveyed by the waterfowl hunting experts:

1. *Wait Until Your Kids Are Ready:*

Don't force your kids to go on the hunt before they feel ready to go. This is a necessary pre-requisite that experts always stress upon.

There's no perfect age when you can assure that your kid is ready for his/her first hunting trip. While some children express their interest in this sport at an early age, there are others who don't feel prepared until quite later.

Just like any other age-specific achievement, it's okay if your kids don't express a hunting desire early on. Don't force them to go duck hunting when they're reluctant. Rather, let them come to you and express their wish to join you in fun. This way, they will be more enthusiastic to learn about the game rules and follow them which, in turn, will end up a hassle-free and enjoyable trip for both parties.

2. It's All about Fun:

They may act clumsy, finding little things too funny, being louder than necessary, getting hungry too often – the list of the things that you may dislike on a hunting trip can go on and on. However, just remember one thing – for their initial trips - it's all about fun and games.

As much as you would like your kids to share your enthusiasm about duck hunting, you need to keep it in mind that, for them, it's an exciting activity – something that they would love to get a dip in. They might not care enough about the number of ducks that they'll shoot down. You may find them a little intimidated by the gun's sound or a bit hesitant to even operate the weapon. In all those exhausting times, just remember, it's an outdoor activity for your children that they are enjoying while spending quality time with you.

A thousand bucks advice here is to keep their imagination as it is. By making the duck hunting trips pressure-free from them at an early stage, you smooth out a path for them to return with you with the same zeal in the future.

They'll ultimately start keeping their hunting score and understand the rules of the games, but that will only happen if they are excited enough to return.

3. Equip Them With An Age-Appropriate Gun:

There's no way for kids to be comfortable in shooting with an adult sized gun. It simply doesn't fit their hands. Get your kid one of the guns from the youth-sized models. For example, a 20-gauge gun from the kid's collection is a perfect size for kids to aim at the ducks.

4. Be Patient:

As easy as it may sound, sometimes you'll find yourself on the verge of losing your patience. There may be occasions when your kid will suddenly announce the need to go and pee, just when the ducks are starting to show up. Or they may get too cold before the birds are even sighted. However, this is the exact time where you will have to remind yourself to take a deep breath and stay calm.

There may be a few times when you will not be hunting anything with the kids, but let's stay focused on the more important task in hand. You are working to instill a deep love for this sport in them, and it will require a lot of patience from your end to achieve this target.

5. Check the Weather Forecast:

Weather-appropriate clothing is a must for your kids to make the most of their hunting trip. They'll never be able to enthusiastically participate in the hunting sport if they feel too cold or too hot. A good idea is to check the weather forecast beforehand and plan their outfit accordingly.

6. Break The Norm – Hunt The Ducks During Summertime:

Although duck hunting is mostly done during the cold weather, try duck hunting during the warm weather, especially when you are taking your kids out on a hunting trip for the first time.

Hunting on a sunny day will give your kids an opportunity to play with the mud, have fun and roam around in the nearby fields. Even if they get wet in the process, it will not be as inconvenient as it would be during the colder time of the year.

Secondly, there is usually less competition if you are shooting during the warm days on a public land, which will potentially lead to more catches.

7. Learn About The Land:

Whether you plan to hunt on a private land or a public territory, take some time learning about its geography and the surrounding areas in a map. It is always helpful to acquire some knowledge about the land to shortlist the areas where hungry ducks will land for sure.

Another tip is to ask the local farmers and huntsmen about the best spots to find the ducks.

These locals always have heaps of information to share, and they love to help.

Not only this, this extra preparation will help you let your kids roam around and explore the nearby fields, which will ultimately make their hunting trip a memorable one.

8. Waterproof Everything:

Especially kids! Children are bound to feel miserable (and cranky) if they are cold and wet. Having a waterproof outwear, including underwear, socks, and boots, is an excellent way to keep them dry and interested in this sport.

9. Protect the Ears With Muffs:

Ear protection (whether earplugs or ear muffs) provide the much-needed protection from the high pitch sound of the gunshots, and they are actually helpful in keeping the hunters focused towards the target by cutting off the noise.

Train your kids to wear the ear muffs when they go out shooting ducks. Thanks to technology, there are now frequency-tuned earplugs available that don't filter off the natural sounds, so your kids won't complain about not being able to hear anything.

10. Scouting for the Ducks:

Don't only go by your judgment, scout and observe the ducks' favorite landing place on a field. There is a reason why ducks prefer a particular spot for landing, and although it might not be one of your favorite places to set up the decoys, it is definitely the most effective place in the field where you will have the maximum chance to catch your target.

11. Empower your kids with responsibility:

Assign them tasks to fully involve them in the process. For example, let them make a duck call when they see a flock nearing by. They may make mistakes, but this is how they will learn.

If you are accompanying older kids, you may invite them to share a bigger responsibility, for example, handling the motorboat.

The bottom line is the more empowered and responsible they feel, the more enthusiastic they'll be towards this lifetime passion.

12. Let them jump and catch the ducks:

Why not? If the kids want to chase the ducks to catch them on their initial few hunts, allow them to do so.

The results will definitely be way less effective

than using a proper decoy, but it will be an excellent chance for the youngsters to learn about the bird's behavior and listen to you when you teach them to layout the decoys the next time.

Chapter 4 - Safety Measures

With the young hunters running wild and free making the most of their favorite outdoor sport, it's a time for you to share their enthusiasm, all the while protecting them from getting into any harm.

Below is a list of some safety precautions that will help you keep them away from the dangers and avoid any mishap:

1. Visit a Shooting Range Before The Duck Hunt:

It will be a good start for your children to learn operating a weapon before they go duck hunting.

Shooting ranges offer a safe environment to practice the firearm's skills and to understand its operation inside out. There are even instructors deployed at these ranges to assist newcomers.

For starters, you can offer your children to use clays for shooting so they understand the gun operation and its handling. However, make sure to arrange the guns that fit their sizes, as they'll unlikely be able to aim the target with an adult sized gun.

2. Keeping the Weapon at a Safe Distance from the Face:

As mentioned in a previous section, it is important to wear muffs for ear protection; however, it's not only your ears that need to be safeguarded.

The eyes are equally vulnerable and in need of protection when you are shooting a firearm. Wear special shooting goggles and always keep the gun at a safe distance away from your face while shooting. Teach your kids the same and get the eye protection glasses for them too. It can only take a flying shell to cause a life-changing damage to the eye in the absence of any protection.

3. Wearing a Life Jacket:

If you plan your expedition at a spot that requires you to cross water, wear a life jacket and get your kids to wear them too.

Anything can happen when you are out there on an adventurous trip; a heavy rainfall, an unpredictable storm or even a catastrophic tsunami. This extra preparedness will cause no harm, but will come in very handy in the face of a real disaster.

4. Respect the Shooting Lanes:

You need to teach your children at an early age to respect the other's territory while shooting. It's not only the matter of goodwill, but firing in another shooter's category can lead to a very dangerous situation if the crossfire injures someone.

A better approach is to shoot within your 10

O'clock to 2 O'clock window to avoid any unnecessary trouble. This is what has been advised by the hunting experts.

However, when you are accompanying children, avoid taking them to a territory where multiple shooters are firing until they are trained and understand the shooting territories well enough.

5. Carry a Waterproof Fire-Starting Kit:

If you get wet while hunting out there in cold weather, you'll immediately need to start the fire and warm yourself to avoid hypothermia; therefore, always carry a waterproof fire-starting kit with you so it could still work in case of an emergency.

Have Your Boat and Machinery Serviced:

All your machinery, including your boat, trailer and motor needs to be in a good working order before you set off for your adventure. The need to have everything in a good working order increases if you are taking your kids along, so get your boat and motor serviced ahead of the adventure.

You can also carry additional batteries and some mandatory spare parts as back-ups to deal with any unforeseen situation.

Using a Boat of an Appropriate Size:

If you plan to go hunting on a lake or a large river, take a boat that could fight off the rough water and is sturdy enough to deal with the big waves. Moreover, never overload the boat more than its maximum capacity.

6. Equip Your Boat With Survival Gear:

Your boat should have all the necessary emergency gear that is required for your hunting trip, for example, a rope, whistle, survival rations, and hand ax etc. You may never require the need to use these extra items, but having them handy in the face of a calamity can make a lot of difference.

7. Treat Your Gun as if it's loaded:

Always imagine that your gun is loaded, even if it's not or when you are unsure about its load status. Additionally, point your gun towards the ground while cleaning or loading it.

Convey these basic gun rules to your children at an early age. Emphasize the dangers that are associated with the mishandling of guns while training them. Also, keep reminding them that they are real guns, and are not toys.

8. Have Your Gun(S) Serviced:

Your firearm is the hero of your duck hunting trip. Coming to know that your gun is out of order after going to a hunting site and laying out the decoys will be a major mood spoiler.

Make sure you have your gun serviced before you set off on a hunting trip. It might also need to be lubricated. If your kids have their own guns, get them serviced too before you go.

9. Carry licenses for all the weapons:

Do not forget to keep the licenses for all the guns that you are taking along with you for the duck hunting trip. You may need to show these at the checkpoints.

Chapter 5 – Animal Conservation

Each territory has its own rules and regulations when it comes to hunting. Waterfowl hunting is no exception. The hunting rules may vary even for the different areas within the same country. These rules are made by the governmental authorities and must be taken really seriously to avoid any penalty. Make sure to learn about them before you shortlist a spot for your hunting game.

Here are a few pointers to help you in the process:

1. *Read The Rules Every Single Time:*

Even if you are a regular hunter, it's a good practice to find out about any changes in the hunting rules every time you are going on a hunting trip.

The hunting regulations normally gets updated

once a year, but any important amendment can be included at any time of the year. It's totally on the discretion of authorities so it is your responsibility to read and comply with them on your journey.

2. Daily Bag Limit:

Each hunting area has its defined bag limit. This means that there is a limit on the number of ducks (or other waterfowl species) that you can hunt on a same day. Going overboard this defined limit can result in a serious penalty.

3. Possession Limit:

In addition to the daily limit, there's a possession limit over hunting the waterfowls if you are planning your hunt trip for more than a day.

Once again, this possession limit varies from one territory to the other so make yourself aware of this limit on your selected area to avoid any unpleasant surprises.

4. Shooting Season and Hunting Hours:

The shooting hours in different seasons also vary. This information can be found on the hunting website of your selected area. Make sure to read about the allowed hours in different seasons and strictly comply with them during your field trip.

5. Permits and license requirements:

Some hunting areas require more permits than others. For example, a federal duck stamp and HIP permit will be required if you plan to hunt the ducks in New Hampshire. Some territories may even require you to arrange a crow hunting permission.

Nonetheless, take your time to learn about these permit requirements and arrange them before you go on your hunting trip. Complete paperwork

permits will help you avoid any
nter with the authorities.

Glossary of Common Terms

Decoy – Something (usually an artificial bird) used to lure or lead target ducks or waterfowl into a trap.

Duck call - An imitated sound (usually a quacking noise) that hunters use to lure the ducks, so they land on the laid out decoy.

Mosquito repellant – A substance, when applied to the skin, clothing, or other surfaces that discourages mosquitoes (and insects in general) from landing or climbing on that surface.

Waterfowl hunting - The practice of hunting ducks, geese, or other waterfowl for food and sport.

Made in the USA
Middletown, DE
06 February 2021